MW00747914

Ordinary
Light

Cynthia Sharp

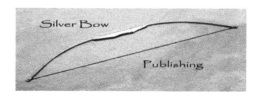

Box 5 – 720 – 6th Street,
New Westminster, BC
V3C 3C5   CANADA

Title: Ordinary Light
Author: Cynthia Sharp
Cover Art: "Paradise Found" painting by Candice James
Layout/Design: Candice James
Editing: Candice James

ISBN: 9781774032534 Print
ISBN: 9781774032541 ebook
© 2023 Silver Bow Publishing

Library and Archives Canada Cataloguing in Publication

Title: Ordinary light / Cynthia Sharp.
Names: Sharp, Cynthia (Poet), author.
Identifiers: Canadiana (print) 20230139965 | Canadiana (ebook) 20230140025 | ISBN 9781774032534
   (softcover) | ISBN 9781774032541 (Kindle)
Classification: LCC PS8637.H3762 O73 2023 | DDC C811/.6—dc23

To everyone who supported my journey

FOREWORD

We live in a complex decade where there is still time. What matters most is embracing the challenge to live simply and responsibility in all our engagements at every level of being. I have some poems like "Tiers" caught in the depression around climate inaction, but I absolutely believe every effort helps.

We're close to the cusp—we live in urgent times, but we're not so far across the line that we should give in to apathy. We live in a crucial moment with the freedom to align with the momentum of hope, to move quickly and peacefully to long-term humanitarian, sustainable green energy. *— Cynthia Sharp*

Contents

petals
shade
texture
light
story

Earth Medicine

when sunlight permeates rainforest winter
and blackbirds ascend from violet bark
soft clouds drift into ancient dragonflies
moving like wind across the sky

on those rare days
when the blue in the raven's wings
shines in the light
go through the open doors

Petals and Roots

I am born
of a grandmother
gentle as pink rose petals
        a grandfather steeped in service
    and ecosystems we thought would survive

born
of Irish and Scottish hope
and generations not comprehending
that carbon dioxide emissions
suffocate great-grandchildren

born
to wild yellow snapdragons
with bright orange centers
and shiny beetles I set free
        oatmeal and quiet
                classic literature and time

Scotland sailed to rural Quebec
big bluestem grasses and isolation
        clover and honey
         wasps I avoid
every element of my grandmother
        beloved Pearl Lang
    where the flowers are from

born
to wild raspberries and blueberries
garden fresh cucumber and wax green beans
cauliflower washed slowly and carefully
the everyday grace of enough
golden lentil soup on the stove
        warm study food
plenty to feed relatives dropping by

                almond-scented hand cream
                we share after doing dishes

14

tea from the kettle
my Great-Grandma Lang would shine
her gift of service to her working
grocery store cashier daughter

winters without plumbing
wearing hand-knit acrylic mitts
that never kept out frostbite
no matter how elaborate the patterns

my grandfather's woodshop I swept daily
waiting with him long mornings
for turtle eggs to hatch in the sand
summer dips in the glacial-fed lake
where he catered to injured fish near the shore
while I baked clay shapes in the sun
or swam with the turtle nearly my size
my tenth birthday honored with a canoe ride
to watch water lilies blossom

I am born
of great-grandmothers in Montreal
wanting me confirmed Anglican
and my atheist science-loving grandfather
telling me I don't have to do anything I don't want to

born
to Canadian-style Chinese food in town
        with extra soy and salt
for rare occasions like my grandma's retirement
        and my graduation

today there are eagles
echoes and freedom
                a planet to protect from the brink
                its hold on me deeper than ashes

Inception

a siren passes
        each wail
                another respiratory silencing
                in an otherwise blue sky
        as pots are vigorously clanged
        in gratitude to healthcare workers

I pause
hope my apothecary medicine
is still at the door
        the four-to-eight-day wait
        for the virus to dissolve from glass

the twice a day pan banging
a catalyst of uncertainty

these times we can't change

people talking too much
        about fear
   when I most need
        calm

only three weeks in
to a year and a half inside

I Just Want It to Be Wednesday

I just want it to be Wednesday
to hear song sparrows on the patio
and watch sunlight move across crocuses
      to honor voices within
       to be calm one day at a time
to live these last few weeks before the end
        to fall in love and finish stories

attempting peace with this resolve
      to live well in lockdown
     grateful for each breath
              blue sky
          hummingbirds
       flowering rhododendron

but every email
every conversation
      is a pandemic alert
     two hundred at once
   pushing PTSD into overdrive

I just want these last days
however many we have
        to be normal
     to bond wholly with them
      each minute and hour
without relentless terror
    and triggers

  everyone rushing
to capture grief in words
   asking for mine

I just want to be present
to this gently unfolding
middle day of the week
     spring verse

the normalcy of Joe across the street
playfully shoveling topsoil in his garden
        to fertilize summer crops
        the possibility that it's okay

permission
        to live simply
        to enjoy the wealth of books

The Diary of Anne Frank this afternoon
        healing recovery breath
handling what we reasonably can
        to cultivate value
with a small number of people

I scoop handfuls of yellow split peas
slowly into a silver pot
savoring each musical ping
and boil them into carrot cabbage soup
with a dollop of real butter
and a sprinkle of Atlantic sea salt

        time for dishes
        the comfort of washing
grateful for electricity and running water
palms and wrists relaxing in the hot stream
with biodegradable fragrance-free soap
        bubbling in the air

the right to calm   to sabbatical
even if only a day   a week   a month
maternity leave for self-care
fewer atmospheric pollutants
this summer a break for Earth
from the intensity of smog

I just want this to be Wednesday
in the sunlight with cherry trees
to curl up in bed with the partner
        I'm still hoping for

and tell him everything I loved
       about our life
clasp hands and remember
all the funny moments of our decades
       knowing we are blessed
        to have shared it all

simple pleasures amid cherry blossoms

Alone and Together
**To my Goddard community
and all our networks that have come together**

I   o p e n   to sky
                         clouds and blue summer
               yield to the peace of lying still
my back eases into alignment; injuries subside
               This life I wish I'd shared with you

I surrender to solitude   creation   writing
lying in wild daisies like I did in my twenties
                    wishing you were with me
               that we hadn't been cut apart

                         it's the kind of day
               mellow jazz music drifts in July windows
                    over neighbors watering lawns
we could almost forget there's a pandemic in Vancouver
               a break between bouts of wildfire smoke
               water shortages and heatwaves for a few weeks
                         an almost normalcy

bird calls open time   mallards   geese   crows
the feathery lilt of cypress in wind
I garden, read, daydream in the hail
of uninterrupted leisure and choice
return to the window, commune with life
and interaction beyond these walls

I dance dreams into plays   existence a learning curve
               starting and ending on gratitude

when the sky cools I look to the sunflections
the glass jars on the counter create on the wall
each one different   catching the light in a unique way
the black cherry jar a mirage of diamonds
now a hummingbird angel

it's one of those days when the clouds break up into millions
an explosion of atoms into universe
and we lay orange lilies on lawns
a tribute to heroes on frontlines

five-hour meditation   perfect for my back
rest   rest   rest   then yoga
the relief of accomplishment
an explosion of bright color, living spirit
oxygen released like worlds bursting forth
breath the sails propelling me along an ocean
let me be longer at peace
hope like islands of grass in the sun

what to do with my perfectly restored meditative energy
learning to keep wellness for health and service to let go

I forget everything else I had wanted to say
just gratitude for real community and purpose
not because there's anything more than this life
but because I value a culture of meaning and kindness

just by being in the world you've taught me so much
about self-acceptance and love
we stretch like dogwood trees, realizing we've grown

voices cycle past my window in the lightness of summer evening
children's calls signal the freedom of not having to be anywhere
the return of time

we're all ordinary these days
and there's something beautiful in that
our regular unstyled hair and selves

accede   bow   stay home   stay safe
let the eagles carry our dreams

breath

early rays illuminate the balcony
slow beginnings of a Monday
hummingbirds remind us
we are part of the peaceful rhythms of nature
there is time for all
                             squirrel pauses
                             a pink lotus opens

monarchs flutter through tall grass
dancing in the light
silver and burgundy strokes of paint on warm canvas
at ease in an outdoor studio
the calling of our bodies to the sea

the poetry of stillness in late afternoon
when the leaves of the Japanese maple
        are tinged with elixir
pearl crescent butterflies alight in aster and lavender
           reminding us it's the little things
             that make up our lifetimes
           breathing each moment of sun
               and now
          the cadence of a day

Sea Dreaming

I celebrate Earth breathing
in this rest from our exhaust
this reprieve from air travel pollution

> give thanks
> for all those safe from the virus
> tasting clean air
> for the first time over Beijing

watch in amazement
as whales glide into inlets
now that we've eased up
on our flurry of noisy boat traffic
and when it's finally safe
walk in sunlight and cherry blossoms

> let sea wind moisturize my skin
> and once again dip bare feet
> in the swoosh of waves over shore

Each Step with the Earth

it starts with a camera
taking me for strolls
teaching me to listen to the stories of flowers

and from my window
on immobile days the clouds
my bedspread a Mexican beach
          journeys inner
each step with the biosphere

          celebration rather than sacrifice
          Easter rather than Lent

          to walk and drink in my community
           to travel great distance on foot
learn the names of local shop owners and baristas
          give thanks for beaches   foliage
                    and clean air most days

bend down to see cappuccino-striped snails
          drinking rainwater
from concave orange maple leaves

help purple starfish back into the sea
          allowing simplicity to heal

Renewal

healing majesty of the ocean at dawn
cocoon of rhythmic eternity
translucent turquoise saltwater waves
how strong your presence in us can be

        touched by afternoon light
        rich buttercup yellow swirls
        amid shades of green in the trees
        the sun upon our dreams

evening arrives with refreshing release
        peaceful bliss of resting
        beside a sleeping child

           little hands
       turned inward
           to our heart
       as if in prayer

       quiet of the breaths
       rain on the skylight
       moonbeam on the sea

Bed of Blossoms

                they give you
         your name on a desk
a little of yourself unbroken

         but what you need
         is all of yourself
         a bed of blossoms
         wholly allowed
         all the time

no longer seeking
         permission
                for biorhythms

Pocket Lint Arrives

To the new literary journal *Pocket Lint*

I inhale the aroma of print
palm its crevices and edges

      breathe in words
      unfold story

hold handfuls of paper
artwork under fingertips

      forget my tea

meaning replaces ritual

Garden Ballerina

the pink umbrella fairy
dances in the sun as well as the rain
strawberry curls at one with the wind

       her three-year-old
       arabesques and pirouettes

ever a poem
      for the fluffy orange tabby
waiting in lavender and chives
       by the clay birdbath

   the day's bright yellow
resurgence of permission to be

Cadence of the Wind

like a cadence of gratitude swirls
        wind moves mist
 across rocky blue landscape
to rest in frosted evergreen

above almond-tinted branches
        winter sits still
in the tips of Grouse Mountain

snowy owls look out over nature
sensing the savory mood of the season
the meandering gift of time
seeing things as they are
and blessing them with love

moon a quarter boat
on the cool mountain river
auburn hair let down

Blossoming

my toes among wild snapdragons
I am a bed of yellow and orange flowers
purple crown chakra in my heart
       blue-green story
     not ready to leave yet

healing vibrations awaken
like manuka honey inside

     all the flowers bud
pink and lemon resonating through me
     the meeting of deep nirvana
     and professional practice

       the sun
   a mandala in the grass

being allowed to value ourselves
      and work
    at every age

Ferrying to Freedom

if I could add a day to any month
I would give it to May
and see Snug Cove tomorrow

I would read *Harry Potter* all morning in bed
inscribe dreams in its pages
then don the coral Italian silk blouse
with billowing sleeves
that I paid too much for
and paint my nails cherry tree floral
with lime leaves

I would breathe spring light
wear pink petals in my hair
and let the wind weave ocean spray
through my curls
as I inhale the aroma of fresh sea salt
ferrying over to forest trails
and hikes through Bowen Island rainforest

      I would taste the starlight
        in royal blue skies
aquamarine blossoms travelling deep in the night
      and live solely on my terms

I Didn't Go Back

I returned instead to green
to seagulls   heron   and sand
    clouds and time
each moment enough

how perfectly aligned I am
after this second visit to the ocean
in eighteen months
the calm to write
communing with shore

even if I teach or tutor again
it will always be as this new self
at peace with natural rhythms
the pace of having walked with the sea

Emancipation

I run through redwood
to rich black earth
absorbing my ashes
rainforest reaping sky
body in sunlight
starlight and trees
growing out of me
dawn and night
eternity in forest
cool air   ferns   cedar
          home

lavender ablaze
mountains gently lightening
nature's morning hymn

Covid Soliloquy

there's something about morning
     and still being here

     how little
we can actually get by on

bathtub laundry
a miracle of simplicity

     how good it feels
     to lie down in the sun
     in clean Italian silk

   a whole bench to myself
     and know I'm fine
     soaking up rays

     to flourish
   in the aftermath

Davis Orchard

in the cyan-misted morn
June shades the veranda
with hearts of branches

longer days and time
iced tea in the green
as the sway of apricot and plum leaves
creates a daytime lullaby

a gentler pace of endurance
knowing each moment
is fully enough

Sunflowers

hundreds of seeds
sustenance and beauty
the ever-changing way
stems bend in the light
a reminder of the magnificence
of life and grace

not only are they alive
but the planet nourishes them
with sunlight and rain

Pomegranate Sunrise

peach and pear sky
     evergreen in gold
         a fresh page of dawn

the way a new story feels
     upon waking

answering the calling that tops all
     frosted in freedom and time
         the sacred act of morning

Sky Flowers

branches mingle into buds
a canopy of butterflies setting sail
the blossoming of talent
from a hidden cove of ideas
the work of the trunks
to manifest largely the kernel within
to dream in blends and bends
of a sea-green world
the magnificence and relief of standing tall

we are fluorescent fronds of tree fish
swimming through phosphorescent foam
to a clear path of what we deserve to be
        the mysticism of color
    aura of forest made tangible

like ancient dragonflies
the esoteric heart of the world
        tasting creation
we embrace permission and freedom
        to go directly
to where we most need and want to be
an island cocoon of love   light   and safety

in the communion of trees we learn
        steadily working
            day by day
        season by season
stretching branches to finally flourish
that self-actualization is for the good of all

our growth protects others
the evolution of consciousness
mirroring meditation

The Temple of Trees

deep inside Cathedral Grove
I morph into the heart of ancient cedar
empyrean resin an open path
to the mysteries of the universe
       veins flow
       leaves fall

gentle curves embrace entropy
spread into earth, the birth canal
we imagine death to be

my ashes journey to rich soil
in the sinewy trunks of redwoods
palpable palms unveiling the paradox
this journey a golden tunnel to the core

   a moon carriage
the whole Earth in its cradle
an embryo to another world
  an inverse cocoon
     spiraling   beyond
        the descent back

Evergreen Altar

stay focused and strong
in the saffron night
ashes sprinkled in soft trunks
of naturally fallen cedar
a realm of rose highlights
sparkling in aurora borealis

shadows won't catch you
if you beam toward radiance
no longer manipulated
by misguided obligation
to enter any murkiness
not meant for you

inhale the auspicious candescence
infused with the scent of conifer
a candle along a pomelo path
to your inner child

stream along starlit stones in forest soil
through blood vessel rivulets
            to dissolution
            the return to nothing
            reborn in light
            arteries pulsating
            universe creating
            destination in sight

flow to the heart
the inner transcendence of trees
            a wrapped mummy
            in womb time bliss
                to eternity
        one with the altar of earth

Sisters of the Meadow

winter bursts forth fairy saplings
        sisters of the meadow
          magical and raw at once
pristine pine tweens dancing safely
persimmon and pistachio holiday tinsel
adorning their natural environment
        roots intact
allowed the depth of their beauty
      incantations of blue
in the stillness of frozen lakes
    quietly into their core
like the brave red fringe of wildflowers

    the undefined graciousness
        of being

Unveiling Light
**Written to Hieronymus Bosch's painting *Christ Carrying the Cross*
with lines from *The Bible***

every generation paints Christ
      in its own image
  restrictions placed on good
what it feels allowed to embody
   the pressure of the crowd
to enforce handed-down norms

faith solid or wavering
we sculpt our salvation
      in the limitations imposed on us
        an adherence to the binary
when we ache to transcend
      traverse faithful devotion
        to altruistic atheism
blue above heartbreak
      heaven on earth
soft leaves, turquoise
      rounded trees like bales of hay
free of crowds, judgement, groupthink

mild, subservient Jesus
plans for the day still in reach
obedient to God, content
beyond the chaos and misdirection around him
      while walking through it
  the softness of wood and lines
      aching for green
touching an almost memory of self
forgive them ... for they know not what they do
      the ignorance of mob mentality
      the incomprehension of it

the gentleness of color
nescience subsides to knowledge
following the barefooted steps of the teacher
the one who walks in the path of gentleness

simplicity, strength from his God
abiding with the calm of the
pastoral blue and green beyond
the harmful injudiciousness of humans

a species whose stupidity
now surpasses what nature can heal
what it should have to heal
playing ego with nuclear war and planetary fire
      not speaking or acting for truth
the absence of courage amongst the crowd
the disappointing reality
      that though many walk with him
        in the presence of his light
          they are too fearful
  to change the behavior of the guards
to stand up to injustice and the abuse of power

how gracious and ordinary Jesus appears
the revered in all   our capability to be him
to walk with him, as faithful servants to higher good
he makes the path easy, our mission simple
      to follow and trust him
that's what strikes me most, even as an atheist
    my desire to follow the serene Jesus
     walking honestly   aware   dignified

how does the earth feel on his feet
as he treads with respect and appreciation
his right heel at one with the ground
humane in an agitated crowd
       focused on bridging
       heaven and earth
     one authentic step at a time
      the symbolic made literal
where I used to see innocence now strength

the complexity of the layers of analysis
    this Jewish rabbi canonized
        into a mysticism of miracles

that we too find our resistance to oppression
   through humble acts of everyday courage
         grace   for its own human sake

I too look up
to the wind
and mountain
         try to prevent
         Antarctica from melting
                  until the stars take me
         back
                  atoms exploding
                  into new universes

Inertia

I wake
to winter rainbow

      offer a walk
      after tea
      but can't promise

      how can we vow
the universe won't snap back
        into nothing

      yet I wish I'd gone
      in the glint of sun

Mustard Seeds

palms   open palms

to communicate without working to death
no longer opening too much to all the wrong things

       no longer   no longer   no longer

palms   open without burden   open without overworking
      open to self   life   universe

open   without extra weight   open   with boundaries
  direct communication

sway like the branches Christ waved on Palm Sunday
my Palm Sunday   atheist   at home
     in this body   and being

this confused and confusing being
that doesn't know how to feel allowed
to step into all the rivulets I deserve to relax in
       neck   shoulders   heart
     a trinity of star-shaped flowers
       white petals in wind
     palms   open and breathing
     mustard seeds in my fingers

embank this river of too much   grow sturdy   protect
     embank the flow of self-denial
the programming I need to let go
     embank and build

lacuna of love   connection   what I deserve
    my time for myself and calling

when relatives wrest a life path
forever pays the price in lacuna
the children I didn't get to have
the grandchildren I crave daily

the mystery lacuna   a world I want to fall into
                the portal I need
keep dreaming I'm twenty again and haven't been abducted
but the lacunae take you   hold us   contain us
all the opportunities of us over and over
the pattern of giving attention to all the wrong people
at the cost of myself   ever being us   securing us
                the hole in the marrow of us

palms breathe   embank boundaries   let air through
                tiny star petals let go
        this nothingness we create meaning from
        this universe that exploded out of nothing
my life in lacunae in the empty spaces of negative energy
            nubivagant electric moments of us
like looking through the lens of a melted kaleidoscope
                sparked with sorrow
what could have been   will never be   distorted

your lover comes to me in dreams   tells me she understands
grieves with me   the loss of the child she gave up
                before nurturing you
        mothering you   restoring you

still pray my ash and love will reassure you
I had chosen you with everything in me
a response to your having chosen me
that instantaneous moment I call our forever
one spark of connection enough to endure
the ratio of hornets to hummingbirds

mustard sun lightens   feeds butterflies
baltering on the broken remains of loneliness
this deathbed alone   floating only into self
and dreams of what might be

   coconut milk   the real world
  a little bit of time for ourselves
            toward meaning
        peaches and dates

every decade she visits anew
        Mary Magdalene to us
             a strawberry flower
a culmination of all the goddesses in my life
welcomes my love more deeply each time
      sheer kindness   understanding
       we heal each other's losses
       help each other carry them
   as we walk uphill   into clouds
      inflorescences of heaven
   the sky yielding peaches

she's different in every dream
    servant   disciple
  entering our Jerusalem on a donkey
     earth woman love
   this new ascendent strength
    giving sunlight
  to each other's wounds

What We Call Fine

O Sea Air
how I long for you to be enough
to infuse our daily lives with the gentle energy
of authentic being
to extinguish the fires and dissolve the cults
of climate change ignorance
to breathe with you today

today you are enough
your cool voice renews me
allows focus and reading

all at once toxic dryer fragrance intrudes
and I have to close windows and roast

in what world did anyone declare
volatile organic compounds better than you
ionized soothing Sea Air

then continental smoke covers the coast
what we call fine above
the amount of deadly fine particles
no one should inhale

there are lethal pollutants in our air
and we make indexes to categorize it
instead of laws to halt it
the world still fossil fuel addicted
my cough worsening

but Sea Air
you alone are enough
set us free from the
cult of climate destruction
breathe us back to the wisdom of simplicity

The Alchemy of a Heartbeat

as the outdoors fills with smoke
our duplex sways to *Swan Lake*
my eighty-six-year-old neighbor
turns up the record player
to waltz with the ghost of her husband
and I am lifted in overtures
limbs limber in body memory
slippers shuffling pirouettes
our minds inhale music
while our lungs become earth

Mount Vesuvius took Pompeii all at once
in 79 AD but we go slowly at first
more fire and tar each summer
pummeling ourselves with pollutants

people of ancient Pompeii didn't know
they lived near an active volcano
that an earthquake seventeen years prior
and tremors in the ground
as magma gurgled forth were warnings
so they didn't take action
to save themselves
from that noon, August 24 heatwave

but we know that carbon dioxide emissions
escalate climate change
that every war traps heat in the atmosphere
until forests spontaneously burn
longer and harder each year
emitting more carbon dioxide of their own
where once they turned it back into oxygen for us
now conifers burst into flame
with the incalescence of the shared biosphere
while manufacturers ignore the correlation
slow on the urgency required
to reach carbon neutral

ash fills us and we dance
the last few hours on this west coast Titanic
Friday, August 13, 2021
the worst air quality on Earth for us

at night we grieve the demise
of our home and bodies to preventable destruction
this one planet   one Cascadia   one set of lungs

like the noble Pliny
who rescued as many citizens
as he could from ancient Pompeii
then died on the beach of respiratory problems
I wonder how long our bodies have
to struggle against fine particle inhalation

this year the damage
a lifetime of perfect blood pressure
altered to stage one hypertension

smoke and smog
the equivalent of eight cigarettes a day

my pulse in my throat
arteries chewed up
but in the morning with new energy
we give thanks
for all that still is

the glory of clear days

all we remember
and still are

Pyre

her love blazes in my life
beloved grandmother
   how I sacrificed for her desire
     until I stopped
    recovered myself
   went through flames to freedom
now on the other side of the country
    in wildfire

   eclipsed until masks burn away
until my voice is the only flame, then gone into earth
   phoenix we are not
but having spoken our words remain
 a singed orange sunrise
smothered behind a veil of smog

   to speak in these dying days
   parched tongues
   charred paradigms
   how you burn
   controlled and uncontrolled
       devastating
       freeing
       alive
    open mouth
    vernacular ripple
    ring after ring unwound

elephants stand still burn alive
no longer believe they have strength to resist
years of life disappear into oblivion
as our planet heads to stardust
the pause before the next big bang

as the last fire goes out we bury ourselves in words
wrap them around us for safety
sleep in handmade paper
breathe only nirvana

sorrows of lost years dissipate
      voice returns
after the fire that divided our Earth
when jealous adults took too much
her candle extinguished

      I listen for presence
      spirit and soil inhale as one
      quiet quotidian sky

goddesses abide as we invite them
fan the air around them
allow them to emerge within us
she who was everything still with me
how she would prepare oatmeal each morning
lie beside me as I gently awoke
      a communion of being ...
      ordinary light

Burning Times
After John Keats's *Ode to a Nightingale*

i

grief encapsulated with graciousness
        quietly embodies the lotus
sucks my breath as tiny Buddha watches
I cradle sorrow like the child I didn't get to have
        pocket Buddha meditates
disappears into smoke-driven sokushinbutsu

                hammer of trucks
exhaust   noise pollution   dryer chemicals   smog
like it's not enough that the province is on fire
                forty-five degree heat
        Lytton burning   deaths in wildfires
shellfish cooking on the beach   us next
humans start up non-electric cars
                for non-essential outings
                        Friday the thirteenth
        this densely populated city
makes the worst air on Earth worse

beloved wind from the sea   a brief shift in fortune
        accumulated sins dissipate
                as the tar cloud spreads away
mingling with clean air over the ocean
                hummingbirds pause in blue sky
        visit me from the lilies of Beaver Lake
                keep it July
flying and feeding as though it's a temperate summer
        like ones of millennia past
living as though seasons are still tenable
a concept I taste faintly in memory
being outside without burning
lying under the plum tree reading
        decades ago
before the fires reached Vancouver

before air conditioning we don't have
   was required for apartment survival
    more electricity

this civilization killing itself in generative excess

   Stellula Calliope
    how you feast
like these conditions are manageable
 darting in and out of tubular florals
bee balm matching your magenta throat

   you with the freedom
       of not knowing
  perhaps you too will die young
        even die out
  but you grasp each second
unaware of what is being done to us

     sharply present
     all about today

ii

O Royal Pink Throated One
if you could reunite my chosen love and I
the union we solidified forever in my DNA
nights at the Pacific   Kitsilano Beach
lying in sand   cool reprieve
amalgamation enough meaning
          even on the brink of extinction
the certitude I've ached a lifetime to return to
          the balance we bring each other
if your trust in your right to exist could extend to me
              your right to live fully
     your elixir unite me with my partner
the destruction around would be easier to digest
                  our chemistry
          insulate me from traumatic trembling

take me back in time before the abduction
lend us your staying power for a world of basic security
that I may have lived with my chosen mate

          O hummingbird
           amid crows

how I wish to hear the whirr of your wings
rather than polluting planes   than engines
that once represented freedom
now a reminder of the colossal danger of ignorance
the more we ignore climate change the worse it gets

          O hummingbird
     I'd rather hear your softness
        in all your feathery flush

to forget the headlines   triggers
interruption of news already agonizing
          intensified by isolation
but the more people out my window
          drive while we burn

the harder it is to forget
to let go into peaceful evening
to write and breathe and be in the time we have
jolted each instance gasoline motors are ignited
       all day and night
more than one vehicle per family
   more than one time a day
              oil based cars
                towing
           oil based boats

this world a burning playground for the rich
but we are all us and them   innocent and guilty
      our complicity in the wealth addiction
         of the one percent
            winding us to
               congested
                 c
                oll
                ap
                s
                e

iii

this once temperate coast
      now tornados and heatwaves
          biomes and windstorms
vocabulary that once described life now used
      for human-made geography killing it
         the air begs for mercy
evergreens grieve their counterparts
      devoured in other regions
crave eroded intergenerational longevity
      know the sea is not enough
      to drench the fire that is coming

marrow of ancient trees cracks open
gone at once like my beloved grandmother
      and her siblings
         ancestry cremated and lost
           continents burning

industrialization doesn't care   enough
cars still pollute   excess still a lifestyle
I try so hard to be good
      but the world goes to dust anyway
         like the fiery wings of a thirsty bird
      in unprecedented heatwaves
dehydrated with the tears we hold back

my neighbor dies in the heatwave
      an ending too abrupt
forgotten as not enough action connects the dots
      between fossil fuels and death
        the city keeps driving
      disconnected from consequence
five hundred and eighty British Columbian citizens
      gone in a June heat biome
like people dropping dead of asphyxiation
        in Mexico City
    from carbon dioxide emissions in the eighties
      and dying in France in the nineties

from climate change-induced temperature spikes
        when I thought for sure
drastic preventative action would be taken

       where are personal ethics
the will to pay to go solar to save lives
       obtusely martyred good

the incomprehensible apathy to which we all succumb
  the tragedy of the commons now eating us alive
        and I too a sinner having used plastic
            contributed
      to this ten thousand years
    of trapped heat waiting to decay

iv

Calliope in the midst of it all your chorale
              a lotus lifeline
through stems and vines to roots of change
to future great-grandchildren   our apologies
that you face a habitat smothered in smoke

may you still blossom in green energy

these syllables I scrape together meanwhile
        not as free as your melody
but with everything in me just the same
             my lifeline
      choice to continue in serenity
        in spite of everything

I too live as I choose
take time from upheaval and ordeal
     to compose
the rhythms of language   a healing break
     like your torpor of night rest
         poetry my restoration
            lungs still suffering
       but soothed
          in the act of composing
     whether or not my letters reach the future

      a birdsong

         not as free or cheerful
         but a choice to conciliate

v

dusk   dark with charcoal
another round of fumes
threatens to erode the cerulean canvas
                night falls
but the moon remains butter yellow as it should
            rather than infrared
                for now

   peonies and roses perfume the garden
lilies and lavender labor like medicine women
            invisible beneath the stars

eventide sage clears the air over Irish prayer stones
            and I water hope beneath a cobalt heaven
                    a ritual I continue even without faith

        my collected rainwater washes word stones
                in the garden for fairies
    I no longer pretend dwell in the plant pots

        the magic it gives me   a transient joy
the power of kindness to all creatures large and small
            as we are able
                    humble actions matter
                        scent of cedar in each breath

vi

dawn alights and you return to sip nectar
but the sun if not red is still not what it used to be
     still not right British Columbia is burning
          the world is burning
yet we have this reprieve of almost getting to the sea
in eight more weeks I might get to the sea
       beloved and estranged from me
      through sixteen months of
              pandemic
                 isolation

instead I sink into ash
     depressed
that carbon will choke you too

Crimson Calliope
a flurry of meadow
       too busy buzzing for my grief
       for the chaos the planet suffers
         you surrender to now
       embrace afternoon like a squeaky toy
your chirps the highest and best piano notes
      in the midst of Eden in ash

here on the edge of destruction
you're Cinderella, Bambi and fairy tales
but I live in burning times and you do too
      even if you don't know it

Magenta Throated Emerald Chested One
how your shine lights everything around you
      buzzing voraciously
yet all at once it's too much   my checkout cue
     Disney over the top
in this twirling out of control derangement
      your notes too high
             too fast
               tire me

it's not your fault but the background
you are meant for rainforest quiet
to decorate gently and instead
you are whirring as engines rev overtime
it's all too much   not enough citizens see the destruction
    that you belong among moss-covered redwoods
        and ferns absorbing your trills
where you decorate rather than reverberate

pine-needled humus and chanterelles
a porous attenuation   leaves   branches   bark trunks
reducing sound waves with moisture
instead of here where roaring industrialization
       is too loud

windows open all day and night for heat relief
    as we cough up fine particles
with injured throats and ears   everything on overdrive

  how do you achieve torpor so far from home
foliage removed from you and replaced with concrete
    this *'too much'* is where I wear out

    that you go so high and collapse
       because we've poisoned you
      and few see
        clearly enough

like the rubber Buddha on my papers I shut down
    ready to fade into eternal worship
    to meditate in death

   though I know climate change
   will burn devout mummies too

     not even sokushinbutsu is safe
     from the fires
     of oil greed

vii

Calliope thank you for coming back
for staying in Vancouver all seasons
so practical on your mission   your right to life
            as though the world's not burning
if your years be shortened you don't waste them
                  lamenting   grieving
                  the stolen future

you too choke on the air   suffer respiratory infections
                  pneumonia
                        long-term loss

may you take consolation
            knowing my beloved grandmother
                  would be proud of your tenacity
            your enthusiasm for sugar and color
to celebrate what sweet crystalline remains

            b
              e
                l
                  o
                    w

            the blackbirds
observing from high conifer branches
            you land on our lawn
              ravens and crows
the mythological bringers of light and death

                  yet you
            sipping sugary sustenance
                  call me
                  to continue

viii

continue   how do we continue   blend cultures
of consumerism, complexity and internationalism
    with sustainability   cultivate the ordinary
        revere simplicity as a worthy norm
give up jets and pollution   make electric cars affordable
design cities to provide harmony and fulfilment on foot
        redefine purpose to stop making it worse

your anthem finished you flutter to nearby maples
            torpor at last
            rewriting time
              evolution

        and I am left to ask
    why are we selling our demise
if our chance for peaceful survival is an option

            if meaning can be found
                sated in sustainability

purgatory

even in climate change
the missing future morning angles
resonate with traces of Eden

crows ease along fences
    down to the dirt

still breathing
bare tree limbs morph
into dancing stick people

and we give our words
    to the stillborn

Tiers

prepare for disruptions   eruptions   mudslides
       taking out drinking water for weeks
earthquakes as always that one's not our fault
intensified storms knocking out food supply
   and transportation infrastructure
essential bridges demolished repeatedly
      harder each time
          multiple emergencies

      but there's no place to store it all
how do we keep three months of food and clean water
      in a bachelor suite that's flooding
      an apartment that costs more
    than three-quarters of a monthly income

what happens to those who can't afford generators
      how do we function with meaning
when it's all terror   denial   arguing and survival

       this culture of collapse
       addicted to self-harm
      scraping off tiers to the quick
        like a miscarriage

lines so tight they've lost breath
my poetry like my respiration   stunted
chopped too fine   in this pressure   to exist

Saturday night
making space for water supply
giving up books to create room

I just want to nurture myself with novels
      escape into characters
      and a bubble bath

       be again

like a hot spring my cycle waits
for the blood-red moon
synchronizes as I swell with her
to burst into birth
mist of pomegranate in the rain

last chance to give
another email claims
can you give back the use of my hand
to lie down in snow and be free
go to sleep without fear
of economic or climate uncertainty

waiting for something that's gone
summers without smoke
blue sky
chosen partner and future
everything déjà vu
a mixture of novels and dreams

if only I could get back in
to not having to know

it's
the end

Hymn of Existence

i

breath between worlds
symphony invites symbiosis
a landscape of dance
bodies swim through air

delicate chimes   tree lights
us in our twenties in the library
arms of nature   womb of life
potential unearthed
the warmth of sugary cooking

divine spiral of relation
between inner and outer
every sound a psalm
chosen direction
manifestation

ii

first frost grapples
with the paradox of meaning

in this capitalist realm
of loneliness and fear
we're told to build libraries
we're not allowed to store
to make money where there's not any
and to never feel good enough
to be allowed what we want

do my moments of peace
equate enough meaning

iii

decades later I disinter myself
from other people's dogma
trails of skin peeling
like sepals along healed cuts

save scraps of voice
tucked in favorite books
so I won't be discarded

safe in hidden chasms
bound until they wither away illegible
smaller and smaller in the margins

maple leaves reminiscent of Pound's petals
tips of sun across last waving vermillion

iv

the richness of lime against sky
        lichen on bare limbs
the palette of empty oak branches
        stored pigments
           bursting

spring yellow catkins and tassels
the micro-movement of forest

           when we vibrate at its pace
             minute increments
           restoration reclaimed

                gentle array of deciduous mulch
                 belonging

     eagle flies close
     double rainbow
        stars
breath between worlds

Rivulets of Light

hope lights the distance
   rivers of leaf veins
vestibules of the sun's ever presence
aglow like my grandmother's serenity lamp
      in the solitude of gratitude
      a temple of inner nirvana
the reset button for a healthier healed planet

how quiet the world is in concord
this little speck of time that's our life
pinnula rafts set sail to the heart of Earth

     all gifts and paces welcome in daylight
       where afternoons curve softly
        like folds of peach silk
         like time
      with my beloved grandma knitting
        every second together
         all that we need
        the ethics of simplicity
         a rare softness
        in the winter sky

pine in amber-lit December night
sturdies and restores the fractured self
the veins in all things from moths to foliage
        gossamer threads
      weaving the wholeness of our web

        increment
        upon
      sacred increment

Silvered Dawn—A Litany for Concussion

I knew I'd won the lottery of solitude
     delicate chimes
the turquoise of a New Zealand paua
an iridescent spectrum of shimmering soprano
lifting me into the heart of characters
a magic realist dimension of rainforest duet

     new stories a requiem
     to missing memory
     an elegy to the decades
     that sang euphonies through me
     tangerine, lemon, lime
     now sand in the sky
     light from an ended star
     the cantata of elevation
     sparkly frost on a winter beach
     the sea bringing me home
     lavender tears sing
     for colors I no longer cantillate
     an echo of notes
     gone like my grandmother's warmth

for the first time a longer lingering of symptoms
     after this newest concussion
more than gracious forgetfulness and indecision
      longer brain fog silences
     like Beethoven composing deaf
      this too soon folding in

tunes with icicles unfold along a frozen river
a hymn to changing seasons
after the third accident
partnered with a young genius
for an ecopoetry spot in the fall festival
     searching for my words
      at home in hers
the winter sun setting early in rose

I embrace new ways to effloresce
the florescence of stanzas on paper
vibrations that once filled classrooms
    now
   p-u-l-s-a-t-e
   between lines

yet all the laurels I lay on the podium
all the blends of harmony
in autumn hydrangea
all the waves of sea blossoms
     don't stop it
       from being a funeral

Pearls in the Stars
With a line from Hamlet's act 3 scene 1 soliloquy

what is the sound of a star evaporating
a miscarriage trembling through me

Draconid meteors dizzy a cloudy sky
     reach for her remains
evaporate before touching earth

the thousand natural shocks that flesh is heir to

        all in one   she is gone
     her body extinguished

I linger
     as teardrops fall
     through the night
          empty and ready
         for the other side
       I no longer believe in
     and curl into her ashes

her ashes sparkle
in frosted falling starlight
ripple through decades

the softness of quiet after rain
your chair still in the light
long after you've gone

Continuing After Her

the colors of morning
deep beet merging into rich green
the sound of water meeting a teabag

      tasting snow
      sea air
      freedom

        this moment
    purple sky and words
this little heart in sun

On Her Departure

since she left
June roses
shadow the whitewash

cherry blossoms adorn
the gray stone edges
of the birdbath
       mute spring rain
           wait for the world
              to lighten

Phantom Limb

        on winter nights
young couples meet in the pines
       at Spanish Banks
        lives intact
young and protected even at twenty
    with the means to act
   on their personal choices

my life was already broken by then
severed without warning
on the cusp of twenty-one
from my partner   tiny room   and career
my one lucky break with a major talent agency
the means to secure our apartment
forced into a no-show against my will
long before cell phones or internet

the penalty for having trusted
to be cities apart without money or autonomy
       shock and loss in place
   of our budding common-law life
     widowed before midnight
   by abductions beyond our control

now beneath cold demi-moons
my love's DNA thrums through my body
     like a phantom limb
    beyond jasmine city lights
where winter limbers scent sea air
      as liminal lemon silhouettes
        Cranes mated for life

    I dance with my ghost of shadows
     the unfading apparition of us

for everyone with no one to dedicate to

I fondle the silver links
of my peace chain
solid as fibroids
where will my womb go
my desire to nurture children
ropy tissue the longest line out of me
where continuity was meant to emerge
grandchildren to inherit memories
this overachieving uterus
fertile only with clots
I pretend are infants
intensifying endometriosis pain
in the gravity of supermoons
twins I dream as cramps sway
with the pull of binary stars
boy and girl babies I name
sunflower and poppy potpourri made music
but when is it my turn
to nurse lasting connection

my hand on the altar

      snow   dead tissue
the crick   crick   crick of fingertips
      in daily tasks
snapping in frostbitten numbness
   pulse thrumming through
as my heart struggles to hold onto them

icy winter bleeds through peach roses
      crisp clarity a lens

I used to shake fresh snow
out of lime-leaved bamboo trees
   now I rest cut tendons
struggling to restore themselves

overuse of the computer mouse
damage from sanitizing groceries
accidentally repeatedly in flesh wounds

      tingling   electric   numb
          swollen
doctor predicts blue lines are a blood clot
     my hand on the altar
having sacrificed two years of physiotherapy
     to stay home   be part of the solution
     stop the spread of contagious Covid
while we ignore the rest of ourselves
      give up swims   skates
exercise outside the apartment
for the myth of martyrdom

taking the pandemic request to stay home
   to levels of unnecessary sacrifice

      dehydrated veins pray
       to outlive the roses
     not crumple like the basil leaves
      I dried to fight infection

before the confirmation
white blood cell count normal
inarticulate fingers
and a slowed-down body
green veins bulge through wrinkly skin
like aging garlic with bulky shoots
beneath beige translucent peel
weirdly wrapped enclosed cloves
deformed looking
yet a gift of abundance
     free fresh chives
  to add to salad at no extra cost
my stone fingers a blessing too
  of slower days
       time
     just being
     present

I am soft earth
  with the right to live peacefully
    curves of ice and foliage
      my rounded knuckles
        pink and peach sunset
      lighting the snow
    the hope of longer days
   the scent of cedar wafts up freshly cut
promising balance for the rest of the journey

I Embrace

> *I embrace*
the quiet of waiting
sunlight making rings on our fingers
> the ocean on bare fee
waves lapping a sandy shore
a webbing of lace bubbles
wedding day henna across my toes

> *I embrace*
the right to be me
as culture collapses
> your skeleton
imprinted in dust
slivers that scrape and scar

> *I embrace*
not knowing if universes reverse
into oscillations of big bangs
> cosmic uncertainty
> that it is enough
> to be
to have known a glimmer of us

> *I embrace*
the falling of petals
through time   light
in all the ways it refracts

days entirely for calling
being allowed
in all the colors
I am

> *I embrace*
my witchy gray hair
> this long winter of Covid
> when all I wanted
was dream time   uninterrupted

awaiting petals
tendril after tendril
     of soft
         spring
           light

    I embrace
birds in bassinet flowerpots
bond with the evolution of morning

    I embrace
a life dimmed without you
meaning diminished
the moon an eclipse in the clouds
    the time I have left
     my sore body
    long days of light
    last lines of leaves
     harvest lanterns
  camel clouds across azure
 the way daytime gently vibrates
before I succumb clean air   time   sun

the flow of maple leaves
shimmering on branches
  in early November
letting go   at their leisure

    I embrace
  breath in and out
the flap of raven wings a heartbeat
the exhalation of nothing into universe

    I embrace
green ivy in white-capped waves
a solstice offering, a genie's lamp of wishes
like the tail end of a rainbow dissolving in mist
  with the foghorn's permission to rest
a reminder that I'm the one I need to let live

88

   I embrace
a freely chosen adult life
the moon in an artist's palette
hands dipping in water
a rhapsody of flute notes
the way spiderwebs shimmer
   in evening light
     ever in process
       content with the pace

   I embrace
the natural rhythms of a day
cleanse in soothing honey
let pearls of liquid gold drip onto clothes
absorb tiny increments of movement
dandelion seed sailing in sea air
the energy of consciousness

   I embrace
swimming ripples of movement
my relationship with water notes of a symphony

   I embrace
    restoration
float in a spirit world of petals and light
this now of clean air
      blue sky
      snowcaps
    fragrant flowers of time
the way shadows bend
to live gently for its own sake

shade and an empty calendar
the quiet of summer
contours of autumn
night rain under
orange streetlights
feet in warm sand
the view the log us

I embrace
the widening of my heart
self-care a lifetime
with creative galaxies that restore me
the softness of treeless paper
this existence in poetry
evenings when it's still light

the vibrations of your soul
like the fluttering wings of a firefly
electrically alive
as friendship ascends to love

I embrace
winding curves of dream time
rich tangerine reflections
when the Pacific holds the sky
an undercurrent of hymn
this whole long day stretched out
my need to relax and unwind too

open the doors
let the wind through

close my eyes

remember

ACKNOWLEDGMENTS
With Gratitude To

My publisher, Candice James, for always going the extra mile to make dreams come true; my thesis advisor, Juliana Spahr, for encouraging me to trust the writing, enjoy the process and open to new styles; second reader, Jasminne Mendez, for careful attention; our graduate program directors, Danita Berg and Elena Georgiou, for creating such a positive and vibrant atmosphere; poetry/editing workshop instructors Beatrix Gates, Donnelle McGee, Stephen Mills, Richard Panek and Roberto Santiago; classmates Daemond Arrindell, Brooklyn Baggett, Pamela "Jaz" Banks, Robyn Brooks, Fiona Blundell, Maria Burns, Jack Cameron, Caroline Catlin, Suzanne LaFetra Collier, Domenick Danza, Socorro de Luca, Judith Fabris, Marina Flores, Linda G. Hatton of Ink Tracks Editing who copy edited the manuscript, Suli Holum, Heath Houghton, Quintin Humphrey, Alaina Joleen, Yolanda M. King, Amy Landisman, Jaimie Li, Megan Loomis, Rebecca Woods Meredith, Derrick Newton, Charles Poekel, Shannon Rempel, L'Ance Harlequin Rouge, Ari Rubenstein, Masha Shukovich, Alicia Smith, Evan Smith, Margie Stokley-Bronz, Donata Thomas, Miriam Tobin, Wren Tuatha and Jenny Tsai, who helped shape some of these poems; all my Goddard peers for every workshop, reading, study session and Take Ten moment—you are my wings; Ann Graham Walker for introducing me to Goddard; Timothy Shay; Jilly Watson for paintings I wrote to; my many writing communities, with special thanks to Lara Varesi and Sheilagh Macdonald from the Burnaby Writers' Society, Angela Rebrec and the Delta Literary Arts Society, and Carol Johnson and Janet Kvammen from the Royal City Literary Arts Society; Brenda Campbell, Karen Edma, Sharon McInnes, Michele Rule, Karen Schauber, Bonnie Quan Symons, Julie Ann Thomason, Carol Tulpar and Sally Quon for all your support in literature and life; the Chincoteague Island Theatre Company whose pandemic monologues inspired this collection; as well as *Better Than Starbucks, Black Bamboo, Lyric Singers, Pocket Lint, Poetry Pause, Prolific Press, The Miramichi Reader, The Pitkin Review, THE SKY IS FALLING, THE SKY IS FALLING Anthology, The Vera Manuel Award for Poetry* and *Quills Pandemic Edition,* where some of these poems have recently appeared or been performed.

And thanks to **YOU** for reading this book!

Author Profile:

Cynthia Sharp holds an MFA in creative writing and an Honors BA in English literature. She is a full member of the League of Canadian Poets, was the WIN Vancouver 2022 Poet Laureate and was one of the judges for the Pandora's Collective 2020 International Poetry Contest. Her fiction, poetry, reviews and creative nonfiction have been published and broadcast internationally in journals such as *CV2, Prism, Quills, Pocket Lint* and *untethered* and nominated for the *Pushcart* prize. Cynthia served two years on the executive of the Federation of British Columbia Writers and was the City of Richmond's 2019 Writer in Residence. She recently completed graduate studies in ecopoetry in Washington State, where she was on the editorial team of *The Pitkin Review*. She is the author of '*The Light Bearers in the Sand Dollar Graviton*' and '*Rainforest in Russet*' available worldwide.

CPSIA information can be obtained
at www.ICGtesting.com
Printed in the USA
LVHW050020130223
739067LV00002B/4